Searchlight
BOOKS

What Do You
Know about
Maps?

Using

Road Maps
and GPS

Tracy Nelson Maurer

Lerner Publications ◆ Minneapolis

▶ To Ann, who always knows
the best way there

Lerner Publications Company
A division of Lerner Publishing Group, Inc.
241 First Avenue North
Minneapolis, MN 55401 USA

For reading levels and more information, look up this title
at www.lernerbooks.com.

Library of Congress Cataloging-in-Publication Data

Names: Maurer, Tracy, 1965– author.
Title: Using road maps and GPS / Tracy Nelson Maurer.
Description: Minneapolis : Lerner Publications, 2016. | Series: Searchlight books : what
    do you know about maps? | Includes bibliographical references and index.
Identifiers: LCCN 2015039637| ISBN 9781512409529 (lb : alk. paper) | ISBN
    9781512412956 (pb : alk. paper) | ISBN 9781512410723 (eb pdf)
Subjects: LCSH: Map reading—Juvenile literature. | Roads—Maps—Juvenile literature. |
    Global Positioning System—Juvenile literature.
Classification: LCC GA130 .M444 2016 | DDC 910.285—dc23

LC record available at http://lccn.loc.gov/2015039637

Manufactured in the United States of America
1-39541-21245-2/25/2016

Contents

Chapter 1

WHAT ARE ROAD MAPS AND GPS?

This amazing world of ours offers so much to see! Maps can help us find our way. Maps use symbols to represent places and the living or nonliving things there. They let us locate these things in our environment.

This family uses a map while on a road trip. How can maps help us?

Cartographers, or mapmakers, design maps for certain purposes. Some maps mark borders of cities or countries. Others display facts about a place, such as how many people live there. Still others focus on roads and highways (the main roads in an area). These are called road maps. They help people find their way from one location to another.

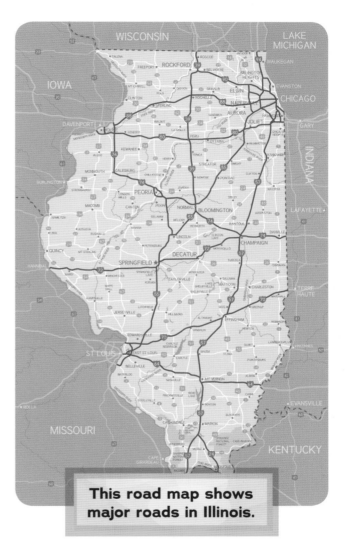

This road map shows major roads in Illinois.

Modern Road Maps

At one time, all road maps were printed on paper. These maps were large and had to be folded for storage when not in use. These days, many road maps are on cell phones and other devices. These maps can change as roads change. For example, if a road were closed for construction, the map might update itself to show that. These maps can also pinpoint where you are by using sensors in the device. Maps like this are part of the Global Positioning System, or GPS. GPS is a system that uses signals from satellites to tell you where you are and to give you directions to other places.

GPS is behind the mapped routes that smartphones plot out.

Early GPS

Satellites are human-made objects that people send into space to circle Earth, other planets, and the moon. They can send signals to devices such as cell phones. Satellites are a fairly old technology. The first GPS satellite launched in 1978 for the military. President Ronald Reagan made GPS free to the public in 1983. Russia, India, China, and other countries hope to launch similar systems.

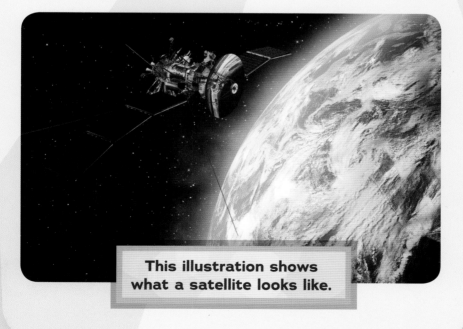

This illustration shows what a satellite looks like.

Helpful Road Maps

Road maps and GPS help drivers plan their trips. Some drivers prefer winding, scenic routes that pass through pretty or interesting landscapes. Others want the fastest route from one location to the other.

Freeways are highways built for fast travel. Drivers might look for routes that include freeways if they want to get somewhere quickly.

If you were planning a trip, you might look for points of interest on a road map, such as campgrounds, national parks, racetracks, museums, or schools. You might discover a historic site or a wildlife viewing area.

Road maps can help drivers find a different route if they need to. Construction zones, car accidents, or other hazards may require changing routes along the way. Road maps come in very handy when your route changes at the last minute! Road maps help travelers in many ways.

Even GPS can't warn drivers about every detour ahead of time!

Did You Know?

Even before paper road maps were invented, people had methods for finding their way around. Many early people used piled stones called cairns as a kind of primitive map. Cairns acted as landmarks. They marked spots where certain natural features could be found. They also showed the way to food and other important resources.

These cairns are in Iceland.

Chapter 2

WHAT'S ON A ROAD MAP?

Road maps use a language of their own. The language includes symbols, special lettering, and colors. You can learn how to read this language. When you do, you'll be a road map pro!

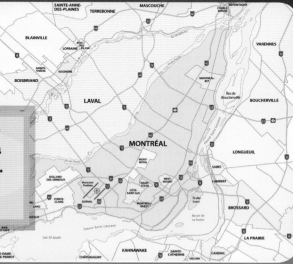

Lines and colors are important parts of a road map's language. What else does this language include?

11

The Compass Rose

Like most maps, road maps often show which direction is which. They use a compass rose to show this. A compass rose is a symbol labeled with the four main directions: north, east, south, and west. Some compass roses are labeled only with an *N* for north.

This compass rose is labeled only with an *N*. East is right, and west is left. To help you remember this, think of this sentence: Never Eat Soggy Waffles.

The Scale

Cartographers use a scale to represent a land area on paper. Land areas must be drawn smaller on paper than they actually are in real life. A scale shows that a certain distance on the map stands for a certain distance on Earth. Scales often look like rulers.

Can you find the scale on this map? Many scales are marked with "miles" or "kilometers."

Boundaries, Towns, and Landmarks

Road maps usually show boundaries, such as borders between states. Most road maps also note towns or cities and some landmarks such as rivers and lakes. Sometimes cartographers use small, thin letters for small towns and large, bold letters for big cities.

This road map uses the largest letters for Austin, the capital city of Texas. It also uses large letters for some of the bigger cities in Texas.

Routes

Road maps show either a network of routes or one route. A network of routes might include all the paved roadways in the United States, for example. GPS typically highlights one route to follow to reach a destination.

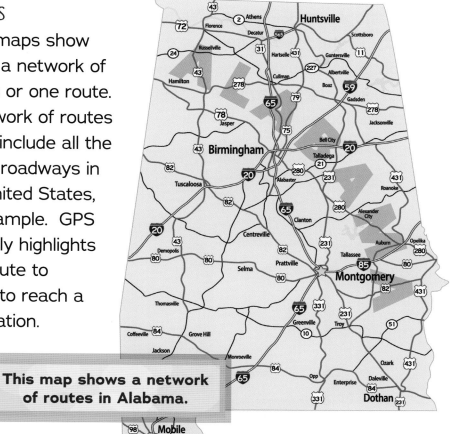

This map shows a network of routes in Alabama.

Lines Here, Lines There, Lines Everywhere!

Road maps and GPS use lines to represent routes. Widths of the lines or colors may show the types of roads. Wide blue lines, for example, could mean freeways. Thin yellow lines may show county roads or neighborhood streets.

A wide yellow line shows a major road on this map. White lines show streets. The blue dotted line shows the route from point A to point B.

Special Symbols

Special symbols often mark the types of roads on a road map. A blue-and-red shield means a road is an interstate freeway. These shields match the road signs that mark interstate freeways in real life. An interstate freeway usually connects two or more states.

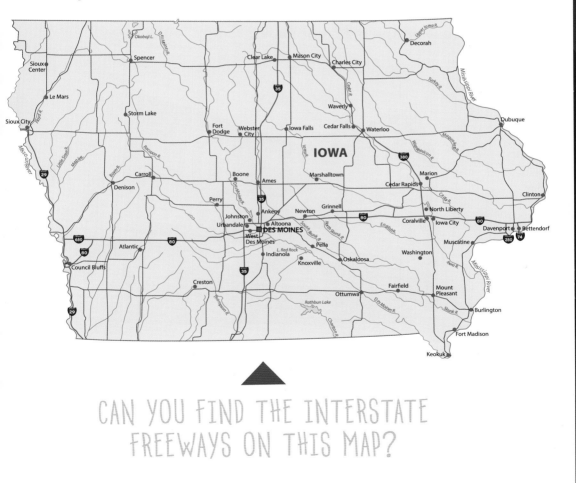

CAN YOU FIND THE INTERSTATE
FREEWAYS ON THIS MAP?

Did You Know?

There's an exception to the rule that interstate freeways connect states. It is Hawaii's Interstate H-1. This interstate freeway does not connect to any other state. It crosses east to west on the island of Oahu.

Hawaii is surrounded by ocean, so its freeways can't go into other states.

Many road maps use black-and-white shields to show US highways. Highways and freeways both often have more than two lanes of traffic. But highways have intersections and stoplights, while freeways do not.

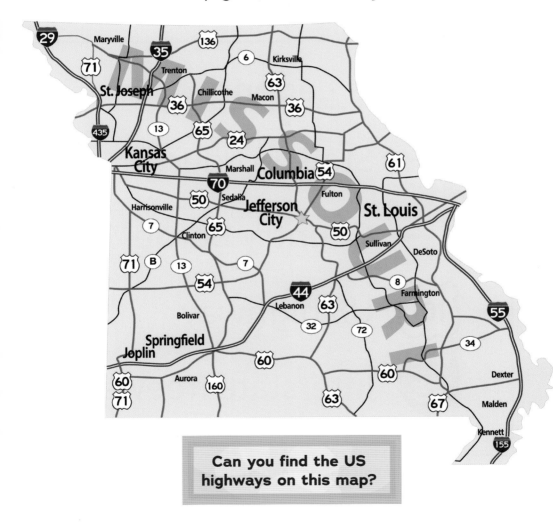

Can you find the US highways on this map?

Cartographers often feature a key, or legend, on road maps to explain what the symbols mean. The legend may appear in a box at one corner of the map. The cartographer may include one legend for an atlas, or a collection of maps.

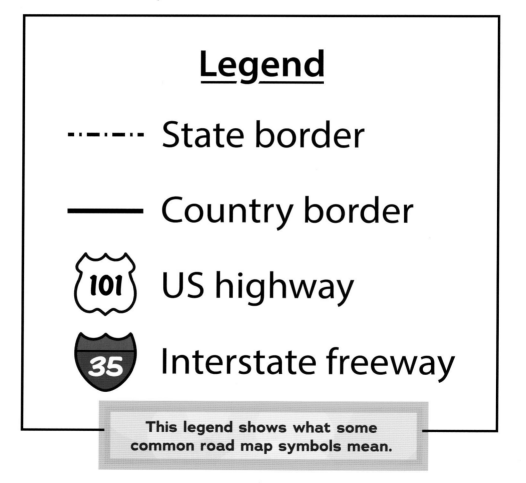

Legend

····-·-·· State border

────── Country border

US highway

Interstate freeway

This legend shows what some common road map symbols mean.

Some road maps work best for certain groups or purposes. A trucking map may show the most direct routes for big rigs. A tourism map may highlight scenic routes or points of interest for visitors to an area. Symbols on the map may show airports, skiing hills, or biking trails.

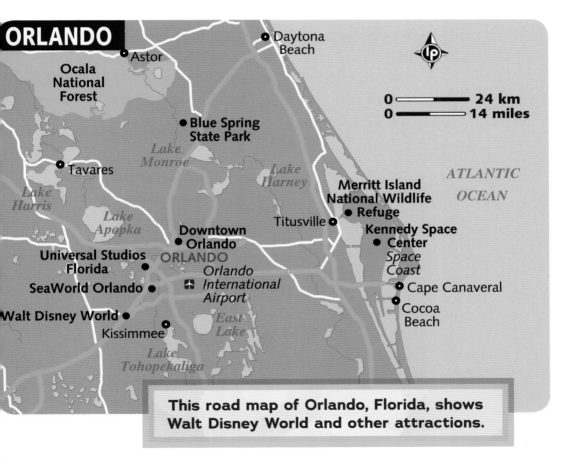

This road map of Orlando, Florida, shows Walt Disney World and other attractions.

Did You Know?

From 1902 to 1927, the number of automobiles operating in the United States jumped from about twenty-three thousand to more than fifteen million! Automobile sellers and other businesses, such as oil companies, made money from this increase in cars. They hoped to get even more people to travel by car. They created road maps to help encourage car trips.

This old car ad encourages people to go on road trips.

Chapter 3

HOW DO YOU USE ROAD MAPS AND GPS?

Using road maps means knowing how to use the tools on these maps to find distance and direction. Special lines that run across some maps can help map users find specific areas quickly. On maps that have these lines, you'll often find a label for each line along the top, bottom, and sides of the map.

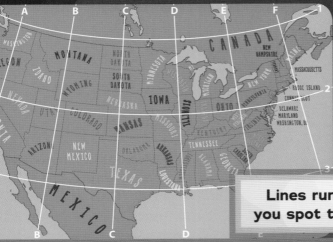

Lines run across this map. Can you spot the labels on these lines?

Try using the lines to find a place on the map below. Say the place you want to find is the Children's Discovery Museum. It is at the point on the map where the line labeled D and the line labeled 3 meet. Find the label for D on the map. Then find the 3. Use your fingers to trace the labeled lines to the point where they meet. You've found the Children's Discovery Museum!

The Tech Museum of Innovation is at the point where line C and line 4 meet. Can you find it?

Using the Scale to Find Distance

Travelers can gauge the distance of a trip using a road map's scale. The map on this page has a scale. Do you see the lines labeled 2 km and 1 mile? That's the scale.

Get out a sheet of paper, a pencil, and a ruler. Mark on the paper where the end of the line marked 0 is. Next, mark on the paper where the end of the line marked 1 mile is. Use the ruler to help you be exact. Line up the 0 mark on the paper with Times Square on the map. Pretend you are there. You want to walk to the Empire State Building. Line up the part of your paper with the 1-mile mark with the label for the Empire State Building as closely as you can. How far is the distance between Times Square and the Empire State Building? Can you walk to the Empire State Building from where you are?

You can use the scale to find the distance between many fun sites in New York City.

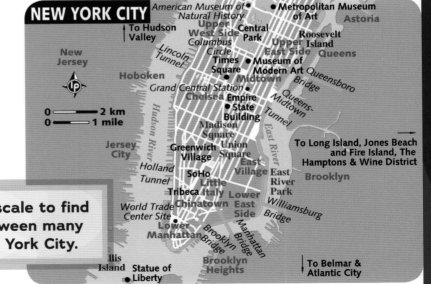

Using GPS to Find Distance

GPS can also show trip distances. Many cell phones have map apps that can help you find your way. A smartphone's GPS detects where a phone user is in the world. Then the phone user can type or talk to tell the map app where she wants to go. The app gives the user directions. It also often lists the distance between the two spots. This can let the phone user know whether she should walk or whether the spot is too far away to travel there on foot.

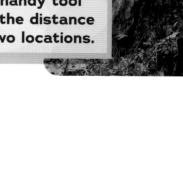

GPS is a handy tool for finding the distance between two locations.

Nothing's Perfect!

GPS is a wonderful tool. But it isn't perfect.
Satellite signals can suddenly drop out. Phone
batteries can die. GPS displays can also distract
drivers and cause accidents. People can't rely
on technology all the time. That's why it's smart
to have a few skills when it comes to reading
paper maps!

Good old-fashioned paper maps
still help travelers in many ways.

Using Road Maps and GPS to Save Lives

Road maps and GPS are great for helping us find places and judge distances. But they can also be used for more serious matters. In fact, road maps and GPS work together to save lives. Rescue workers use these tools to quickly reach people in trouble. Road maps can help rescue workers find their way through unfamiliar areas. GPS can pinpoint very specific locations after streets, buildings, or other landmarks have disappeared in an earthquake, flood, or other natural disaster.

MAPS CAN HELP RESCUE WORKERS FIND PEOPLE WHO MIGHT BE IN DANGER.

A Powerful Signal

In the 1990s, scientists learned that GPS signals bounce off water. This knowledge helps meteorologists, or scientists who study the weather, to do their jobs better. Meteorologists can now forecast storms and check wind speeds even in a hurricane!

Technology helps meteorologists do their jobs.

Using GPS for Fun

GPS can also be used for fun. Have you heard of geocaching? It is like a worldwide treasure hunt for GPS users. Geocachers hide millions of small containers, or caches, around the globe. Then other geocachers use their GPS to find the caches. The containers hold a logbook. They also might contain toys or other small items that finders can take. When someone finds a container, he or she signs the logbook. That way, others know that he or she was there. The person also might take some goodies from the container and add something new. Then the container goes back into its original hiding spot.

Geocaching is popular among people of many different ages.

Road maps and GPS help rescue workers, science professionals, and everyday people alike. They guide travelers on short errands and long trips. Some people claim that the journey is as important as reaching the destination. What do you think?

Has GPS or a road map ever guided you on an adventure?

ARE YOU A ROAD MAP AND GPS WHIZ?

You know a lot about GPS and road maps. Now let's test your knowledge. It's time to take a virtual trip!

You'll be using maps like this on your virtual trip. If you lived in California and were driving to Florida, what states might you cross?

Say your family wants to take a trip from coast to coast. You live on the West Coast. Which highway might you start on? Which ones might you take to bring you all the way across the country to the Atlantic coast? (Note: This is *your* virtual vacation, so your starting point can be anywhere on the West Coast, and your ending point can be anywhere on the opposite coast. Just as long as you choose highways that take you to the East Coast, your trip will be a success!)

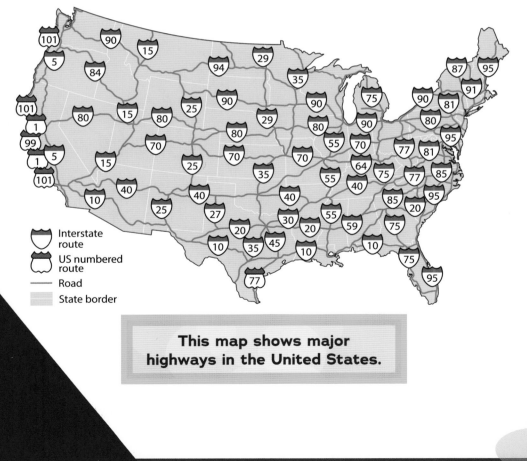

This map shows major highways in the United States.

Now say that your travel goal is to visit at least three national parks on your way from coast to coast. Plan your trip. Which roads will you take this time? Again, you can pick any starting point and ending point that you like. Just make sure your starting point is on the West Coast and you end up on the East Coast.

This map highlights just a handful of the many US national parks.

KEY:

⬭ Interstate route

⬭ US numbered route

🌲 National park

—— Road

▨ State border

GPS displays streets and points of interest, just like road maps do. What are some other similarities between digital and print maps? What are some differences? Do you think one system is better than the other? Why? Which one would you prefer to use on your virtual trip from coast to coast?

Some people prefer to use GPS on long road trips.

You Did It!

Way to go! You understand how road maps and GPS can provide directions and guide your travel. These tools can help you plan short trips or long vacations. How else can you use road maps and GPS?

KNOWING HOW TO FIND YOUR WAY IS A SKILL THAT CAN TAKE YOU ANYWHERE!

Fun Facts

- Any direction can be at the top of a map. Some early maps showed east at the top, because the sun always rises in the east. Pioneers in the United States traveling to the western frontier in the nineteenth century often used maps with the West on the top.

- GPS first appeared in automobiles around the year 2000.

- Each GPS satellite orbits the planet once every twelve hours at 12,500 miles (20,116 kilometers) above earth. Each one flies at about 7,000 miles (11,265 km) per hour.

Glossary

app: a program for a smartphone, tablet, or computer that performs a specific task. *App* is short for application.

cartographer: a person who makes maps

freeway: a highway for fast travel

highway: a main road

intersection: where two or more roads meet

legend: an explanatory list of symbols on a map

satellite: a human-made object that people send into space to circle Earth, other planets, and the moon

scale: a tool that explains the size of a map compared to the actual place it represents

scenic route: a route that provides beautiful views

Learn More about Road Maps and GPS

Books

Kenney, Karen Latchana. *World Geography through Infographics*. Minneapolis: Lerner Publications, 2015. Geography fans will love this fun, visual look at the geography of the world.

Matteson, Adrienne. *Using Digital Maps*. Ann Arbor, MI: Cherry Lake, 2014. Explore more about the maps we find online and on smartphones.

Quinlan, Julia J. *GPS and Computer Maps*. New York: PowerKids, 2012. Learn more about GPS and electronic maps in this book.

Websites

Enchanted Learning: Geography

http://www.enchantedlearning.com/geography
Check out Enchanted Learning's geography page for a compass rose printout, interactive map-reading activities, puzzles and games, and more geography fun!

GPS.Gov

http://www.gps.gov/students
This site provides information and links to videos and other resources about GPS.

Smithsonian: Time and Navigation

http://timeandnavigation.si.edu
Discover more about navigation, including using GPS, with this interactive learning resource from the Smithsonian.

Index

Photo Acknowledgments

The images in this book are used with the permission of: © iStockphoto.com/IPGGutenbergUKLtd, p. 4; © iStockphoto.com/crossroadscreative, p. 5; © iStockphoto.com/hocus-focus, p. 6; © rottenman/Deposit Photos, p. 7; © trekandshoot/Deposit Photos, p. 8; © dbvirago/Deposit Photos, p. 9; © Mgodden/Dreamstime.com, p. 10; © Lesniewski/Dreamstime.com, p. 11; © squarelogo/Shutterstock.com, p. 12; © GrabMaps/Shutterstock.com, p. 13; © Lesniewski/Deposit Photos, p. 14; © suwanneeredhead/Deposit Photos, p. 15; © alexey_boldin/Deposit Photos, p. 16; © Rainer Lesniewski/Shutterstock.com, p. 17; © cleanfotos/Shutterstock.com, p. 18; © Stacey Lynn Payne/Shutterstock.com, p. 19; © Laura Westlund/Independent Picture Service, pp. 20, 23, 24, 33, 34; © Lonely Planet/Getty Images, pp. 21, 25; Chevrolet ad courtesy of Flickr/Michael IFHP97 (CC BY-NC-SA 2.0), p. 22; © Aigarsr/Dreamstime.com, p. 26; © iStockphoto.com/Christopher Futcher, p. 27; © Petunyia/Dreamstime.com, p. 28; © Dr Mike Hill/Getty Images, p. 29; © tirc83/Getty Images, p. 30; © Hero Images/Getty Images, p. 31; © Bardocz Peter/Shutterstock.com, p. 32; © Randy Duchaine/Alamy, p. 35; © iStockphoto.com/SerrNovik, p. 36.

Front cover: © Laura Westlund/Independent Picture Service (map); © iStockphoto.com/cloudnumber9 (GPS); © iStockphoto.com/Devaev Dmitriy (background).

Main body text set in Adrianna Regular 14/20.
Typeface provided by Chank.